D0500510

UNIVERSITY OF MINNESOTA

PAMPHLETS ON AMERICAN WRITERS • NUMBER 102

Theodore Dreiser

BY W. M. FROHOCK

UNIVERSITY OF MINNESOTA PRESS • MINNEAPOLIS

Printed in the United States of America at
Jones Press, Minneapolis

Library of Congress Catalog Card Number: 72-619529
ISBN 0-8166-0645-5

PUBLISHED IN THE UNITED KINGDOM AND INDIA BY THE OXFORD UNIVERSITY PRESS, LONDON AND DELHI, AND IN CANADA BY THE COPP CLARK PUBLISHING CO. LIMITED, TORONTO

THEODORE DREISER

W. M. FROHOCK is a professor of French at Harvard University. Among his books are *André Malraux and the Tragic Imagination*, *Rimbaud's Poetic Practice*, *The Novel of Violence in America*, and *Style and Temper: Studies in French Fiction*.

Theodore Dreiser

IN ADDITION to his eight novels, Theodore Dreiser's work includes four books of short stories and sketches, four about travel, two of autobiography, one of poems, one of plays, and four, best described as miscellanies, in which he mixed science, more autobiography, politics, and social problems. But we read the rest of his writing mostly because it illumines the novels. They are his claim to greatness, and it is on them that any attempt to assess his achievement must fix attention. Current criticism tends to honor him most for *Sister Carrie* (1900) and *An American Tragedy* (1925), assigning second best either to *Jennie Gerhardt* (1911) or to the first two parts of his "Trilogy of Desire," *The Financier* (1912) and *The Titan* (1914); much less is said in praise of the third part of the trilogy, *The Stoic* (1947), or of *The Bulwark* (1946); and of *The "Genius"* (1915) more critical evil has been spoken, probably, than good. We have only recently begun to concede what the Europeans have told us for years, that the achievement these novels represent was truly a major one.

Current manuals credit Dreiser with "power" and "compassion" and they are right, just as they are right in adding that often the power is "crude" and the compassion "mawkishly sentimental." But such formulas label without explaining. The source of his originality was a trait of character: he was constitutionally unable to say he saw what he did not in fact see, what wasn't there to be seen. His drafts show him trying to restrain this gift — for example, in revising *Sister Carrie*, to avoid offending current taste he worked to make his heroine less promiscuous and less willing to be kept than he had originally conceived her — but such attempts failed because the gift was instinctive and visceral.

This naive innocence of vision in his novels made a shambles of the public moral assumptions of his time.

People were supposed to be guided by conscience, but the lives he observed, including his own, were shaped by the blind, incomprehensible "forces" of nature. Everyone agreed that success came from grit, enterprise, honest industry, and clean living, but in his experience the successful were those who combined the most ruthless wheeling and dealing with great good luck. Happiness was supposed to reward deep love and devotion to one woman – with book, bell, and candle – but he learned for himself what his heroes confirm, that the woman we love today may become tomorrow's millstone. Unselfish devotion and kindness were recommended to all women, but he couldn't see that they had lightened his mother's burdens, and they bring little but grief to Jennie Gerhardt, whereas the girl who keeps her eyes open doesn't necessarily come to a bad end because she goes to bed with other women's husbands; witness Carrie Meeber. Such discoveries may strike us today as rudimentary, but the point is that in Dreiser's time no one was supposed to make them. Hence the impact of his novels.

American mores have changed so much that our cultural history seems unreal. It is hard for us to believe that the so-called Genteel Tradition was not a cynical conspiracy among an established elite to legitimize their fortunes and justify the society they headed. Thinkers like Max Weber and Thorstein Veblen have persuaded us so thoroughly that the ethic of the rising and expanding middle class was what the middle class needed to believe that we forget that millions of people did in fact believe in it as they believed in the gospel from which they thought it derived. For many readers, even so late as the Coolidge administration, Dreiser was denying the meaning of their lives.

The fairy tale doesn't report that the child who dared speak of the emperor's nakedness became a popular hero; and although the moral and religious issues that once made dispassionate discussion of Dreiser's work difficult have long since disappeared with the cant that surrounded them, our praise is too often limited to the niggardly admission that he "told the truth" about American life as he saw it. Yet a reader who believes that a characteristic function of the novel is to penetrate appearance and reveal the reality beneath is in no position to dismiss Dreiser so summarily. And if he also agrees that when the reality revealed is important ethically, socially, or culturally, the novelist who reveals it must be granted a kind of importance also, then he must concede a certain stature to Dreiser. The reality itself may be unpalatable – although this is less likely today than when the novels were new. And we may have little taste for the ways and means Dreiser used in the revelation – as is more than likely since we have become so aware of fictional technique in the interim. The achievement isn't thereby explained away.

No one contests that Dreiser knew the kind of American life he wrote about at first hand. Few novelists have written their own experience into their novels with so little transposition, or made it so clear afterwards (see *Dawn*, 1931) that they have done so. (He had to abandon an early draft of *An American Tragedy* because he had poured so much of his youth into that of his hero as to knock the story out of proportion.) Life in America, as he knew it, was absorbing but also rough, harsh, and often nasty.

His father, John Paul, had immigrated from Mayen on the German Moselle, not far from Coblenz, and moved across the country from job to job, doing reasonably well at the weaver's trade until fire destroyed his woolen mill in Sullivan, Indiana, and he was injured by a falling beam during the rebuilding. Nothing he touched thereafter prospered long; he devoted the rest of his life to paying his debts, and retired into what the younger Dreiser considered a very superstitious and bigoted Catholicism. Responsibility for the family, which increased with dreary regularity, fell largely on Sara Maria Schänäb Dreiser, the Moravian farm girl John Paul had married on his way west. The children were Paul, the minstrel and hoofer, who changed the spelling of his last name to Dresser and wrote songs like "On the Banks of the Wabash" and "My Gal Sal"; Rome, who became an alcoholic bum; Emma; Sylvia; Mame, who like Emma got an early reputation for promiscuity and, later, ran a whorehouse; Theresa; Al; Theodore, who was born two years after the father's accident, in Terre Haute, on August 27, 1871; Ed; and Claire. With such help as she could get from the older ones as they left home, the mother dragged her brood from Sullivan, to Terre Haute, to Vincennes, back to Sullivan, to Evansville, to Warsaw (Indiana), and to Chicago, according to where chances looked best of keeping them fed, clothed, and alive. These wanderings assured Theodore an insecure childhood.

The family was never in one place long enough to establish itself, even had it had money to do so. The behavior of the older sisters rapidly earned it the kind of name that meant exclusion from the society of such rural, or semi-rural, communities. Schooling was erratic: Dreiser saw enough of parochial schools to leave him with a lifelong aversion to nuns and priests, and had one experience of a public school that was luminous by comparison. Later, one of his teachers paid his way through a year at Indiana University. He had few friends and few ways of making any. The first volume of his autobiography, *Dawn*, pictures an uncertain, rather unhappy little boy, and then a sensitive, awkward, and no happier adolescent, "on fire with sex."

His novels would be the richer for this life. His uninhibited sisters were material for *Sister Carrie* and *Jennie Gerhardt*. The weak failure of a father and the courageous, responsible, and drudging mother recur in *Jennie Gerhardt* and *An American Tragedy*. The uneasy, unhappy boy, ashamed of his parents and of the way the family lives, and deprived by birth of the pleasures other children seem born to, is embodied later in Clyde Griffiths, the hero of *An American Tragedy*. In addition to such easily recognizable patterns, the fear of poverty and failure that pervades the novels comes straight out of an underprivileged midwestern childhood.

Once he was old enough Dreiser was off to Chicago on his own, employed at first at such jobs as dishwashing in a greasy restaurant or driving a laundry wagon, but in time finding newspaper work on the *Daily Globe*, where he began what turned out to be a long and slow apprenticeship. Wherever he went more experienced hands taught him what they knew. From Chicago he moved to St. Louis and jobs on the *Republic* and the *Globe-Democrat*. Then he drifted slowly eastward, looking for a place to settle down, with stops in Grand Rapids, Toledo, Cleveland, Buffalo, and finally Pittsburgh, where he found a job on the *Dispatch*.

He was training his eye. His early pieces were not momentous journalism, but they show an alertness to the picturesque, especially as it emerges from a drab urban background. He was as fascinated by what goes on in back streets and alleys, away from the glare and glitter, as by the lives of the wealthy under the bright lights. He learned what a newspaper writer so rapidly learns: not to trust his reader's power of inference or his ability to understand what he isn't told explicitly. Less rapidly he learned the value of feeding his reader a diet of concrete facts.

In the Pittsburgh Public Library he read Balzac, who gave him an example of what the novel could be, and a model from which his own fictions would rarely depart. In *Dawn* he regrets that the discovery didn't come sooner, at Indiana University, but one wonders whether Balzac's great value for Dreiser would have been available except for the latter's own previous experience with writing. The Balzac he discovered was clearly not the visionary, "metaphysical," author of *Seraphita* and *Louis Lambert*, but rather the one most apt to teach a feature writer what to do with his material—whose long, factual, third-person narratives, told by a narrator who sees and knows everything, could be accounts of real lives in the jungle of contemporary society. Novels like *Lost Illusions* are built from accumulations of detail that sounds as if directly observed, with the flow interrupted only by essay passages in which the novelist impenitently breaks off the story to explain motives and comment on the action. Elaborate techniques are absent, or else hidden; and Balzac often appeals to contemporary scientific theory to illumine the ways of his characters. Years later, sophisticated critics like Joseph Warren Beach, mindful of the divergent ways of Balzac and James, would reproach Dreiser for being too like his master. They were entirely right in identifying the relationship: Dreiser owes far more to Balzac than to Zola or the other French naturalists, for example. But was Balzac such a bad master to adopt?

After Pittsburgh he joined his brother Paul in New York. In 1894 newspaper work was hard to find. He caught on as a "stringer" with the *World*, but found that the money paid per inch of space wouldn't keep him alive, and moved to a staff job on *Ev'ry Month*. Plainly he had become a hack, and as a hack he soon took to free-lancing articles for periodicals like *Success*—a curious publication dedicated to fostering the great American cult. His interviews with tycoons follow a required format such that one wonders why Dreiser, himself, wasn't embarrassed. The facts are that he wasn't, that material success would never cease fascinating him, and that what he learned at this time would be most useful when he came to write his novels about Frank Algernon Cowperwood.

In 1898, to his permanent chagrin, he married. Sara White was attractive, somewhat older than he, like him from the Midwest, but unlike him disposed to social conformity. Dreiser says that after his first ardor he cooled rapidly but married her anyhow; the union was doomed from the start. They separated after a few years, but even after the separation became permanent, Sara White – "Jug," as he called her – would never consent to divorce and the marriage stayed on the books until her death. In his novels, Eugene Witla (the "genius"), Cowperwood, Clyde Griffiths, and – seen from another angle – Lester Kane in *Jennie Gerhardt,* all commit themselves to women and repent at leisure.

Meanwhile, early in 1900 he finished *Sister Carrie.* Frank Doubleday, the publisher, heeded the enthusiastic recommendation of his editorial reader, Frank Norris, to accept the manuscript. What happened next has been disputed. Dreiser's prefatory note in later editions says that Mrs. Doubleday was so shocked by the story that she urged her husband to withdraw from the contract and that when Dreiser held him to their agreement Doubleday honored it in the letter only, printing and binding the book indeed but making no effort to promote it.

Recent studies find Dreiser's account somewhat one-sided. Doubtless the Doubledays did discover that they had taken on a shocking book, and quite possibly Mrs. Doubleday was no woman to approve of Carrie Meeber, but they may also have had second thoughts about what the public would accept and buy and simply decided to cut losses. In any event, the record shows that they did publish the book and sold, in 1901–2, about 900 copies. It was, at the time, a failure.

Failure haunted, just then, this author of success stories. His marriage was going badly; he was restless and depressed; he worried about his health and even his sanity. In 1902 he got so low that his brother Paul stepped in and sent him to a rest camp operated by William Muldoon, a reconditioner of businessmen, trainer of boxers, and figure in the New York sporting world. Muldoon's rigorous discipline and some fresh air eventually got Dreiser back to a point where he could cope with life. But he left the camp only to find a job at hard, physical labor on a railroad crew, and not until late December 1903 did he return to his familiar setting — and then not as a writer but to fill a series of editorial jobs.

Successively he was on Frank Munsey's *Daily News, Smith's Magazine,* and the *Broadway Magazine,* of which he was briefly managing editor. Finding that he was better at editing than at managing, he moved in 1907 to the *Delineator.* There he was well paid, and apparently found work and surroundings congenial. When his hero, Witla, in *The "Genius"* reaches a similar point, Dreiser clearly thinks him a success. Some even feel that, if Dreiser had remained so comfortably situated, he might never have finished another novel.

But, in 1910, the mother of Miss Thelma Cudlipp objected so vehemently to Dreiser's attentions to her daughter that she packed the daughter off to Europe and got Dreiser fired from the *Delineator.* In the same year he and Sara White completed their separation. The year following he published *Jennie Gerhardt.* The next fifteen years were to be his period of incessant productivity.

After *Jennie Gerhardt* came *The Financier, The Titan, The "Genius,"* the short stories, plays, essays, one of the autobiographies, and finally, in 1925, his fifty-fourth year, *An American Tragedy.* Dreiser didn't write easily, and his drafts show that he labored over the revisions. These must have been years of unremitting work. The reward wasn't, perhaps, the literary equivalent of the success he had admired, studied, speculated about, and doubted in other men, but he had reached material security, his books were read — perhaps more often read than admired — and he had become a visible public figure. He had also forced the reading public to accept serious, grim realism.

Sister Carrie is undeniably a serious and grim story. Carrie Meeber finds life in Chicago as harsh as it ever was back in Wisconsin, and learns that no one cares much whether she starves on what she can earn in a factory. Money and commodities are what count, and the men she meets teach her that physical attractiveness is a commodity, fully negotiable. There is no moral conflict and she isn't bright enough to be cynical; she just exploits the one commodity she has.

She lets Charles Drouet, the salesman she meets on the train from home, set her up in an apartment. She quits him for Hurstwood, the manager of Fitzgerald and Moy's prosperous saloon, who steals his employer's funds, abandons his wife and family, and runs away with her to New York. While Hurstwood's fortunes decline, she parlays her small talent, and her good looks, into a career on the stage, and eventually cuts him loose. He goes downhill to a suicide that is literally a pauper's death, while Carrie, when last seen, is on her way to further fame and fortune.

If Dreiser had made her a calculating little vixen who stopped at nothing to get what she wanted, the story would not be half so effective. In the finished version she isn't even really promiscuous, and none of her moves toward secure ease is really planned. She moves in with Drouet because she doesn't want to go back to Wisconsin, and leaves him again because she suspects that he won't ever put through the "little deal" that would let them marry: Hurstwood has something more substantial to offer. Her conscience nags her, but never loudly enough. She drops Hurstwood, in turn, when she sees the luxuries other women enjoy. She is not even particularly shrewd.

Her men are almost as passive as she. Drouet picks her up on the train because it isn't in him not to try to pick up a pretty girl. Having a pretty mistress, and being known to have one, flatters his vanity. But he is nowise disposed to entangle himself permanently, so that the same instinct that made her attractive to him in the first place now warns him off. Poor Hurstwood is also a creature of circumstances. His marriage has cooled, and his wife is dominating, grasping, and shrewish. Naturally—as

Dreiser knew from experience — he is drawn to any girl who promises to renew his youth, and can be had. Yet he sees the attendant inconveniences, and blind luck makes his crucial decision for him: he is still not sure that he will abscond and take Carrie with him when, as he is closing his firm's safe for the night, he is tempted by the sight of so much money and takes out a sheaf of bills to fondle it; he is still listening to an inner voice telling him to put it back when the door of the safe snaps shut.

Chance plays a similar role in *An American Tragedy* when the accident the hero has planned to bring about takes place without his actually causing it. In both novels the protagonist's responsibility is incomplete; and in both what Dreiser thought of as natural "forces" push them into the situations where they are so vulnerable. Luck combines with nature to determine their fates.

One can see how Frank Doubleday may have despaired of selling *Sister Carrie* in a country where belief in moral responsibility was fundamental. Yet Dreiser was working from life. His sister Emma had come from the country to Chicago, and had formed a liaison with one L. A. Hopkins who, like Hurstwood, had stolen money so that they could run away to New York. Emma hadn't had Carrie's subsequent success, but in other respects Carrie is no more an invention than is his picture of the mean life of poverty she wants to avoid at any cost. The life of the urban poor he knew at first hand; he had been jobless in Chicago himself and knew the skid rows of a half-dozen cities; some of the pages in *Sister Carrie* are lifted almost verbatim from Dreiser's early newspaper sketches of more or less picturesque misery. A strict moralist could condemn Carrie and Hurstwood, and also condemn Dreiser for not condemning them, but he could hardly deny the authenticity of their story.

His reading had convinced Dreiser that there must be "laws" by which the "forces" governing our lives may be seen to operate, and these laws must be open to scientific explanation. Hence a basic determinism in human affairs. Yet at the same time, we must have some degree of free will, at least a limited liberty of choice, or else life is meaningless. He pondered the dilemma for forty years without reconciling the opposites to his final satisfaction.

At this point the difference between his naturalism and that of Zola and the French is fundamental. Zola felt that he was demonstrating the applicability of established scientific law. As he had gotten it from Taine, heredity, environment, and the historical moment determine human behavior, so that he could write, case after case, the "natural history" of two interrelated families under the Second Empire. The formula was already in existence when he began writing, and was entirely familiar to his audience, so that however monumentally wrong Zola may have been in accepting it, he had the advantage of not having to explain it in his fictions. He could take it as a datum.

Dreiser is in exactly the opposite position. He is demonstrating nothing. From *Sister Carrie* to *The Stoic* he pictures life with all the faithfulness he can muster, but casts about gropingly for explanations. They are often inadequate, to a point that such notions as his theory of the "chemisms" that determine personality, or of the electricity that passes from one person in love to the other, are best taken as metaphor. And because he often seems unaware of the inadequacy, his disquisitions may strike an irritable reader as pompous ignorance.

If a naturalist is a writer who treats humans as products of nature, and nature in turn as the seat of the "forces" that shape life, and if in doing so he leaves the impression that nature means more to him than art, then Dreiser was indeed a naturalist. Taine had written that vice and virtue are chemical products like sulfuric acid and sugar; and Dreiser says in *Dawn* that with a slight change in the mixture of body chemicals his brother Paul would have been a great man. Such parallels are endless, and make the point irrefutably. But it is not from a theoretical naturalism that Dreiser's novels derive their power.

Once the reader of *Sister Carrie* has seen the characters and knows their situation, he knows what will happen. Even before Hurstwood's luck snaps shut the safe door, we are sure that he will steal the money and that from that point we shall be following the trajectories of two lives, one still climbing, the other always pointed downward. The inevitability of the outcome is in the characters themselves: Carrie will go on being Carrie, and Hurstwood has already made his own ruin. There is no tragic acceleration of events. Time, as measured by the clock and the calendar, will be inexorable.

Sister Carrie may be classified as objective realism, but beneath the surface one suspects a basic personal fantasy. In Hurstwood, but for luck, went Theodore Dreiser – and who knows how long luck will hold? Dreiser had not exorcised the memory of his unhappy, ineffectual father. Attentive students have detected symptoms of fundamental insecurity even in his endless pursuit of women, believing that he was really looking for the warm protection against the consequences of failure that one woman, his mother, had once given him. The articles written for *Success* are implicit reminders that success does not exist unless its opposite exists also.

Carrie Meeber's success must be compensated by Hurstwood's decline. He must lose his investment in the saloon he has bought into in New York, must try only feebly to find other income, must sink to living on the twelve dollars a week Carrie earns as a chorus girl, must grow shabby and old before our eyes, must go from one mean job to another meaner one, and finally to wretched illness and suicide. One remembers that at that moment Dreiser was headed for a nervous breakdown of his own.

Thus his sympathy for Hurstwood – the first manifestation of his celebrated compassion – may be interpreted, and perhaps discounted, as indirect self-pity. In any event, it differentiates him at one more point from the European naturalists, whose dispassionate detachment was their hallmark. In *Sister Carrie* his pity is muted, but Dreiser is already the man who years later, when he saw the 1931 film of *An American Tragedy,* burst into tears.

Most of the perennial objections concerning technique apply as well to *Sister Carrie* as to any of Dreiser's later novels. His omniscient point of view permits him to tell us what kind of people his characters are instead of letting us see them in action and decide for ourselves. Too often he characterizes them by describing externals, as if all one needed to know about a person were revealed by his dress. Sometimes he puts a terrible strain on credibility: how, for example, can Carrie be so dumb as to want Hurstwood to marry her when she knows that he is already married? What the characters say reveals little that we do not know already; he reports the event and then what was said during the happening, so that the dialogue doesn't, as (say) Hemingway's dialogue does, advance the story.

Much of this kind of criticism boils down to saying that Dreiser was blissfully unaware, in 1900, of the prescriptions that Percy Lubbock would propose as precept, following the example of Henry James, in *The Craft of Fiction,* in 1921. Just how does it happen that a novel written without benefit of such wisdom can affect its reader so deeply? One possible answer could be that in the house of fiction there are several mansions.

Jennie Gerhardt again draws upon Dreiser's family. Jennie's father is a poor, disabled, aggressively religious (but Lutheran, not Catholic), unassimilated immigrant. A drudging mother courageously struggles to keep the family going. Jennie, as passive a character as Carrie Meeber, and not half so lucky, is modeled upon the sisters Mame and Emma.

Working with her mother in a hotel in Columbus, Jennie

catches the eye of George Sylvester Brander, the junior senator from Ohio, who is moved by her sweetly simple ways and good looks. He helps her bedraggled family, overrides her father's surly objections, and says he intends to marry her. More out of gratitude than love Jennie goes to bed with him. Then, before he can make good his promise, the bad luck that besets Dreiser's protagonists intervenes: Brander dies suddenly. Jennie finds herself pregnant, has her baby secretly, and in time goes to work as a maid in an important Cleveland family.

A friend of her employers, Lester Kane, son of a rich Cincinnati manufacturer, finds her compellingly attractive, but has no intention of marriage. From love, this time, Jennie accepts a liaison and lives with Kane in Chicago for a number of years. Even after he learns that the child she has been providing for is her own, Kane seems perfectly satisfied, but Jennie's peace is troubled by the disdain of neighbors who detect her status. Then Kane's father dies, and he learns that to inherit his share of the business he must end the liaison. In time Jennie persuades him that he should do so and he subsequently marries a widow of his own social status. One sorrow is heaped on another when her child dies of typhoid. And then Kane himself dies, and Jennie last appears, unrecognizable through heavy veils, following his funeral at a distance from the legitimate mourners.

This is what the poor may expect of life. In all senses but the technical, Jennie is a good woman – kind, loving, loyal: she has been helpful to an unresponsive family; she even takes in and cares for the old father who once wanted to put her out of the house; she is a good mother to her child, and devotedly faithful to Kane. The latter does not leave her in want, but otherwise her goodness has to be its own reward. Like the heroine of Flaubert's *Simple Heart*, she has loved without return.

Perhaps she is too good to be true. She learns little from experience, and, the complete opposite of Carrie Meeber, she lacks all instinct of self-protection. Her beauty and charm must be taken on faith. (They captivate Senator Brander, but thanks to Dreiser's preference for telling us about character instead of exhibiting it in action, we aren't prepared for his being swept so easily off his feet.) Poverty and bad luck don't embitter her as they do her brothers and sisters. Dreiser was probably combining certain traits of his sisters with some of his mother's in an idealized portrait. In any case, it is certain that Jennie, in his eyes, is an innocent victim of life's injustice.

Here another American myth is punctured: not only do girls like Carrie sometimes not have to atone, but sweet and kindly girls like Jennie can suffer just because they are too poor to protect themselves. Is it possible to be poor and moral, too? The question dogged Dreiser all his life. The impulses that in his later years involved him in such liberal causes as those of Tom Mooney, the Scottsboro boys, and the striking miners in Harlan, Kentucky, go back to his instinctive hatred of poverty. It seems clear that even his joining the Communist party, shortly before he died, was not based on conversion to a theory. He was not a systematic social thinker, and there is much to suggest that his espousals and allegiances were more emotional than rational. He simply disliked seeing strong people push weaker people around.

As Walter Allen insists in a famous study of English fiction, it is characteristic of the novel to protest against the abuse of power. For Dreiser as for Dickens, power and wealth are synonyms, and poverty exposes people to coercion. The poor man has fewer social and moral options: Jennie's brother Bass lands in jail for stealing coal from the railroad – but the alternative would be to let his family freeze. It is a measure of Hurstwood's degradation that he scabs in a motormen's strike because he has no other means of earning two dollars a day. Jennie has the looks and good nature to make Kane an attractive mistress, but not the culture and education to make her acceptable to him, and his family, as his wife. Very little, here or elsewhere in Dreiser's writing, is revolutionary. The word "equity," which he uses so frequently, means little more than that extremes of poverty and wealth are unfair, and that a society that tolerates them should be reformed.

Jennie Gerhardt is not, however, a social tract. Dreiser's aim is less to stir indignation than to evoke pity, and to do so simply by drawing the contours of a life. As in *Sister Carrie*, the structure of this novel is the simplest possible, following the lines of a biography. Time is again treated as rectilinear, the mere unwinding of the years. He feels no need of sophisticated craftsmanship.

He is relatively indifferent to writing in "scenes," and entirely capable of using an entire chapter to discuss what has happened earlier, without advancing the action a step. A more typical procedure starts a chapter with a discussion of a situation or the state of a character's mind; then may come the narration of a new event, perhaps followed by the dialogue that accompanied it; finally there may be summaries of the effect of the event on one or more characters. In terms hallowed by recent use, "report" often replaces "dramatization," and the "authorial voice" is persistently audible, while the "point of view" is entrusted to one character or another to suit the novelist's convenience.

It is in the discussions, where he speaks in his own voice, that Dreiser most clearly confirms the criticism that he writes "like a rhinoceros." The following, from the opening of Chapter 11 of *Jennie Gerhardt*, is not an unfair example: "It is curious that a feeling of this sort should spring up in a world whose very essence is generative, the vast process dual, and where wind, water, soil, and light alike minister to the fruition of that which is all that we are. Although the whole earth, not we alone, is moved by passions hymeneal, and everything terrestrial has come into being by the one common road, yet there is that ridiculous tendency to close the eyes and turn away the head as if there were something unclean in nature itself. 'Conceived in iniquity and born in sin,' is the unnatural interpretation put upon the process by the extreme religionist, and the world, by its silence, gives assent to a judgment so marvelously warped."

Such a mixture of circumlocution, inversion of adjective and noun, uncertainty in vocabulary, and burdened syntax identifies the self-taught writer. Dreiser tells us that in childhood he had read whatever he could get his hands on, but the English and American romantics he goes on to mention, especially when not offset by generous amounts of the English Bible such as sustained Crane, Norris, and even Sherwood Anderson, could be bad models for a style. In addition, the son of an immigrant workman and a Moravian farm girl who learned to write from her children's copybooks can't have heard simple, idiomatic English at home. Dreiser writes an acquired language. So did Joseph Conrad, but it is one thing to write an acquired language, as Conrad did, after having mastered another in the natural way, and something quite different to write one starting as Dreiser did, so to speak, from zero.

The critical moaning over the defects in Dreiser's English can be overdone. His barbarisms are notorious, and it is quite true that he is at times embarrassed to find what Flaubert called the *mot juste*. But it will be noticed that the passages most often quoted to discredit him are those in which he speaks directly to the reader, in his own voice. At the worst they show him being overelaborate, wordy, perhaps pompous, sometimes even arch. In other words, he shared the difficulty with elevated style that characterized his generation. Even Stephen Crane was forced to fall back upon the treasury of pulpit oratory and Fourth-of-July cliché for the loftier passages of *The Red Badge of Courage*. Dreiser's style was formed in the climate of the "Cross of Gold" speech, as the least respect for historical contexts obliges us to remember. He was born too soon to belong to the generation who solved the problem of elevation by avoiding it and adopting the tones and rhythms of *Huckleberry Finn*. And even where his prose offends he is never frivolous; his seriousness and sobriety are evident; however awkward, he means what he says.

Pity is the presiding emotion in *Jennie Gerhardt*, and the emotion is unmixed. The uncomplicated nature of his disposition toward his heroine may indeed explain why this novel should be so simple in outline and, except for the curiously blurred final chapter, so relatively rapid in the narration. On the twin patterns of success and failure, which he had adumbrated in *Sister Carrie*, his feelings were far more complex, and his subsequent novels dealing with them become correspondingly more deliberate in their pace.

Dreiser did not equate success with the mere jingling of millions. Even in his hack-writing days he had included among the specimens he interviewed for *Success* a few who, like John Burroughs, had reached the top without amassing money. In *Sister Carrie*, young Bob Ames, who speaks for Dreiser, explains to Carrie that some satisfactions are not for sale. In various novels Dreiser disdains a number of cautious, conservative, upward-bound types who devote their lives to making as much money as possible at the least possible risk. Lester Kane's brother who runs their family business, Clyde Griffiths' cousin waiting to inherit his father's factory, Orville Barnes in *The Bulwark*, with his fears that his sister's behavior will compromise his own career, are treated without sympathy. Dreiser's aversion to such fellow travelers of capitalism was total.

What interested him was the uninhibited, freewheeling paragon of unleashed energy, the "buccaneer" capable of taking whatever he wanted against any opposition. For such men success is a kind of game played as much for the mere winning as for any tangible prize. In that this figure obeys no rules but those he makes for his own convenience he has something vaguely Nietzschean about him; he also has some of the lineaments of a romantic hero, condemned to operate in the world of business.

Some critics argue that this ultimate descendant of the Romantic Outlaw appealed to Dreiser because the novelist could easily identify with him, as he had for opposite reasons with Hurstwood and as he needed to do with all his heroes. They point out that after *Jennie Gerhardt* Dreiser devoted his life to variations on the rags-to-riches formula, and view his tycoons as examples of wish fulfillment. The argument is plausible: daydreaming has served many novelists well. But it is also true that Dreiser used the success-failure patterns for exploring character in a way that transcends the interest of success and failure in themselves.

Charles E. Yerkes had been a traction magnate who, after making and losing fortunes by manipulating the finances of street railways in Philadelphia and Chicago, had narrowly missed taking over, just before his death, the underground tube system of London. He had bounced back to relative respectability after a term in prison, had been as flamboyantly spectacular in love as in finance — he had retained a law firm to come to terms with his abandoned flames — and might also have gone down in history as a great philanthropist if death had not interrupted his public benefactions. Yet if Yerkes is remembered today it is because Dreiser took him for the model of Frank Algernon Cowperwood. He researched Yerkes' biography with great care, and the trilogy parallels it closely.

Cowperwood is not, surely, a human type found only in America, but just as surely he is one that flowered to fullest perfection in the favorable climate of the expanding American economy. He grows up around Philadelphia, exhibiting all the thrift and industry recommended by the Quaker tradition but untouched by the corresponding moral restraints. His eye for the main chance discovers an opening in street railway stocks, and before he is out of his twenties he is a man of substance, with wealth, a wife who is a cut above him socially, and a lovely home. But his acquisitiveness, which is the expression of his restless energy, is unsatisfied and as his sophistication grows with his wealth he develops a knowing eye for art and women. He takes for his mistress a young and beautiful girl, Aileen Butler.

Trouble comes when a crash in the market following the Chicago fire catches him short and he is unable to cover his losses. He serves a prison term for embezzlement, and gets out, wiser and cannier but fundamentally unchanged, in time to pull together his fortunes by taking advantage of another crash – Jay Cooke's. He resolves to make himself a new life in the West.

At the beginning of *The Financier* the youthful Cowperwood stops to watch a lobster in the tank of a fish market window eat a live squid. This, he realizes as he meditates the revolting performance, must be the law of life: the lobster eats without compunction and will in turn be eaten by a creature further up the scale. Cowperwood's subsequent career bears out the law. Dreiser does not make him a wittingly cruel man, but one whose instincts will not let him be bested in the struggle for survival. Latter-day readers may feel, more simply, that Cowperwood has the personal and social morals of a lobster, but in Dreiser's perspective he is only obeying the law of his own nature, which derives from the law of nature herself.

In *The Titan* Cowperwood has left Philadelphia for Chicago, where Aileen marries him as soon as his first wife agrees to the divorce foreshadowed at the end of *The Financier.* New operations in public utilities – first illuminating gas and then traction once again – multiply his wealth. He collects art and women, the latter recklessly: an unbroken succession of mistresses includes wives and daughters of close business associates. Aileen, whose social inadequacies have made her a liability anyhow, discovers Cowperwood's philandering, beats up one lady in a vulgar brawl, and eventually drifts into affairs of her own. Finally, knowing that they will never crack Chicago society, Cowperwood installs her in an ostentatious mansion in New York.

Meanwhile, Cowperwood's stock-watering, sharp dealing, keen foresight, and sheer nerve make him a national power. He squeezes adversaries, bribes politicians, and buys elections until he seems ready to get control of all the surface transport of Chicago. But at last he comes up against a man of principle who won't be bought, and who is the governor of Illinois. He vetoes the bill that would grant the long-term franchises Cowperwood needs to consolidate his holdings — and the legislature fails to override the veto. Although still enormously wealthy, Cowperwood has to give up Chicago as a bad job.

This "Trilogy of Desire," as Dreiser called it, was to be completed by *The Stoic,* but he delayed too long in reviving his hero, and the novel, published posthumously, can't be judged as one would judge a finished work. Cowperwood's last foray is his try to take over the London underground. Bright's disease interrupts it and he comes back to New York to die. The museum and hospital he had planned as his memorials are not realized, and a flock of legal vultures rapidly pick his fortune apart.

The Stoic further complicates the moral ambiguities of an already ambiguous story. The rapid crumbling of Cowperwood's fortune suggests that Dreiser may have come to feel that his tycoon's whole life illustrates the vanity of vanities. In addition, the concluding chapters increase the uncertainty by following Cowperwood's last mistress to India in search of a guru who can tell her the meaning of life. What the lesson is can be the object of disagreement, but this unworldly man surely does not tell her that the good way to live is identifiable with Cowperwood's.

James T. Farrell, an admirer of Dreiser and one of his literary executors, reports that Dreiser was so uncertain about *The Stoic* that he asked Farrell to read the manuscript and advise him. Farrell attributes the move to the old man's doubting the survival of his talent, and doubtless this was most likely. But one wonders also if Dreiser, in later years, hadn't lost some of his sympathy and admiration for his hero, and perhaps his taste for the values Cowperwood represents. Had he become aware of the moral ambivalence of the earlier sections of the trilogy?

For Cowperwood is, clearly, a malefactor of great wealth. In his private life he pulverizes the Decalogue – except that he does not commit murder – and gets away with doing so because he is rich. In the public sphere he is indefensible: ultimately his dividends could only come from the pockets of the little people who paid more than the ride was worth to get back and forth between home and work. But Dreiser's eye is resolutely turned away from the social damage a man like Cowperwood causes.

Dreiser sees him covered with glamour, richly dressed, handsome in a "leonine" way, and somewhat bigger than life. Cowperwood's great moment comes when, having brought a financial crisis on the other traction enterprises in Chicago, he confronts a meeting of the bankers who have supported them. Thinking that he is short of liquid funds, they tell him that they will call all his loans. But he has foreseen exactly this move, and his position is completely solid. He faces them down, saying that he is ready to pay every penny if they insist. But, he adds, if they do insist, he will "gut every bank from here to the river." Dreiser's admiration here seems complete.

One obvious explanation is that during the years after he left the *Delineator* to return to writing, Dreiser was privately trying the mantle of success for size. This is inescapable in the case of Witla, in the autobiographical *The "Genius." The Titan* and *The Financier* may be read as a portrait of the artist as a success of another kind. For Cowperwood forces his way over the "moralists and religionists" who exist to frustrate the superior individual.

Cowperwood wins through by doing what Nietzsche calls becoming what he is — as much a product of nature as the lobster in the tank. So much the worse if this makes him one of the strong who push about the little people whom Dreiser momentarily forgets. Cowperwood can't imagine failure, and doesn't know what insecurity means. When he wants a woman he takes her, and the women are happy to be taken. He refuses to let marriage become a trap, and summarily unloads women who stale on him. Friends he doesn't need, so long as he can buy lieutenants who are faithful through self-interest or fear. What luxury he wants he simply buys. He even ends by finding the perfect mistress for an old man in beautiful, young, clever, charming, educated, and above all devoted Berenice Fleming. These are, one notes, rewards nature hadn't lavished on the novelist, but just as, but for luck, he might have been a Hurstwood, so also, with a slightly different mixture of chemicals in his body, he might have been a Cowperwood. Even a self-proclaimed realist may dream occasionally, especially if, as Dreiser does in *Dawn*, he proclaims in the same breath that he is a romanticist by temperament. Few of us feel responsible for the morality of what we dream.

A reader brought up on more recent fiction may feel the defect of the trilogy to be one of technique. As always, Dreiser is following the example of Balzac — but, in this instance, somewhat inattentively. Balzac is perfectly relentless about stopping his narrative to tell his reader in advance what the character on display is going to be like. But when Balzac arrests the narrative flow of, for example, *Le Curé de Tours* to give us the "physiology" of the Old Maid, and tell us what to expect of Sophie Gamard, Mlle Gamard goes on to do exactly what we have been made to expect. "Action is character," wrote Scott Fitzgerald in one of the notes found with the manuscript of *The Crack-Up*. "A man is what he does," echo the existentialists, following André Malraux. The obligation a novelist incurs, when he discusses a character with his reader, is to remember that what the person does characterizes him also, and the two ways of characterization had better not contradict each other. Quite simply, what one sees of Cowperwood in action disagrees with Dreiser's estimate of the manner of man he is.

The fault is not completely Dreiser's, however. Cowperwood may be fascinating as a full development of the potentials of a certain human type, but culturally he is a museum piece. Little could be more foreign to us now than his world of unregulated business, and few or no inhibiting taxes, where the public conscience was less offended than overawed by the Robber Barons. The best part of the trilogy is set in the time of Dreiser's own youth; the streetcars Cowperwood modernizes are still drawn by horses and the big deals he brings off are of the gaslit, horsecar era. A time that prefers security to free enterprise must read these novels as historical fiction, or else out of interest in Dreiser.

Interest in Dreiser is necessarily the best reason for picking up *The "Genius."* Whereas the Cowperwood story is fictionalized biography — the kind of fleshing out of verifiable fact with unverifiable, imagined detail that the French call *vie romancée* — the life *The "Genius"* puts on public display is his own. An element of self-justification, as in most such more-or-less veiled confessions, creeps in, along with a tendency to touch up and correct the details of his own destiny.

Eugene Witla grows up in a midwestern town, but in a family less desperately poor than Dreiser's and not driven to the grim expedients his own adopted. The boy is sensitive and shy, but not made to feel painfully excluded from the life around him. His sisters don't embarrass the family, and his father, though not an imposing figure, isn't a bigot or a walking ruin. In other words, Dreiser makes Eugene's a less special case than his own.

Young Witla drops out of school, where he has not done particularly well, works awhile for the town newspaper, and then moves on to Chicago. There his lessons at an art school bring out the wisp of talent he has suspected in himself, and determine his vocation. There also he has his first experiences with women, including an easygoing model at the school, and then Angela Blue, an attractive, farm-bred girl, somewhat older than he and a deeply conventional nature. When he leaves Chicago for New York he and Angela are somewhat vaguely engaged to marry.

Marry her Eugene finally does, but after his work has begun to attract attention, and after he has come to know young women more cultivated and interesting as well as less conventional than Angela. His early success in painting continues, but he becomes weary of the conformity of his bride. Angela Blue is Sara White, of course, and the story continues to parallel Dreiser's own – though with certain adjustments – through breakdown, temporary loss of belief in his gift, increasing estrangement from his wife, a job on a magazine, and dismissal from the job when he becomes too attentive to the daughter of an influential family.

The "Genius" isn't one of those novels in which the protagonist learns the difference between appearance and reality, and finally comes to some triumph of self-understanding. Witla seems no wiser about himself at the end than at the beginning. His feeling – clearly Dreiser's also – that an artistic temperament entitles him to exemption from the rules of normal decency and fairness that ordinarily govern conduct, not only in sexual behavior but in social and business activities also, is hard for the reader to share. There is something too self-centered and priggish in the callous way he terminates his liaison with the model, and not much less in his relations with Angela. One gets a feeling that where there is so much ego there should be more talent.

Dreiser wrote most of *The "Genius"* in 1911, while his mind was also occupied by Cowperwood. (His publisher of the moment advised delaying publication.) Cowperwood is as exempt from the rules as Witla, so far as actual behavior is concerned, but he asks for no special treatment beyond what he can force the world to give him. The closest he ever comes to self-righteousness is when, in *The Titan*, he tells Aileen, who has caught him red-handed, that he can't change what he is and that she had better put up with him. The quotation marks in the title of Witla's story may be ironic, but the irony isn't based on a perception that Witla's values are rather confused. As a self-portrait, *The "Genius"* is too self-indulgent.

For the satisfactions Witla wants from art are those that Cowperwood wanted from business: money, luxury, women, position, perhaps even power. On this scale, Witla's gift for painting comes perilously close to falling in the same category as Cowperwood's proficiency in watering stocks.

Outside the context of its moment, *The "Genius"* doesn't seem a particularly subversive book or one to endanger public morals. But on the eve of World War I disquieting reports were abroad that revolt against the reigning mores was sweeping such bohemias as Greenwich Village. Young-lady poets were writing poems about burning candles at both ends, and young artists, back from Paris, were full of new and alien ideas. Very naturally, Dreiser's novel came to the attention of John B. Sumner and the other custodians of virtue. Probably no novel in which sex played such an important role could have escaped, but *The "Genius"* was only the more challenging because it was so serious. Dreiser was no smart aleck to be dismissed as merely frivolous. Such a book had to be suppressed. The total effect of suppression was, of course, to advertise the novel and increase the notoriety of its author.

Thus *The "Genius"* is a modest part in the history of the conflict between Artist and Philistine, American style. Despite its defects it does reveal the awkward situation of the painter or writer — at a point in history when "alienation" had not yet become a cliché. Subtler minds than Dreiser's, from Veblen on, had made many of the same points and analyzed the causes more deeply, but no one else had made such an attempt to show what could be the consequences on an individual life.

Meanwhile the conception of art that emerges from Dreiser's discussion of Witla's work adumbrates the aesthetic of his own fictions. Witla's preferences attach him to the Ash Can school. He likes subjects suggestive of the color, roar, and rattle of the great city, such as earlier painters avoided as inherently ugly — streets on rainy nights, the clutter of crowded squares, freight yards with massive cars, glistening rails, and mighty locomotives. He goes in for strong, if not violent, color, broad and sweeping effects, and the feeling of motion and activity. In brief, as Dreiser puts it, he painted "Life." With due allowances for looseness of language, the identification of art with life is the basis for a realism from which the picturesque is not excluded. There is much talk about "the beauty of life," also, in his autobiographies, as well as the assumption that the power to feel this beauty marks the "poet." In Dreiser's literary practice this can be reduced to the statement that the observation of life as actually lived can be the source of strong emotions. The formula suggests that his realism, as he remarked himself, was romantic.

Only a romantic realist could have written *An American Tragedy*.

Critics agree generally that out of all Dreiser's novels this is the one with which we are most obliged to come to terms. It is either a literary monument or a monumental failure. Over the years readers have come to perceive that *An American Tragedy* is a shrewdly planned structure of calculated effects, that Dreiser knew what he was about, and that little if anything gets into it by chance. It is immaterial, for example, whether or not he borrowed the questions and answers of an actual courtroom dialogue for the trial of Clyde Griffiths; what is material is that the pages sound, and are meant to sound, like a transcription. They have the exact value of an account based on a stenographer's record. Either one grants the validity of the technique or one doesn't. Whichever the decision one's grounds will be ultimately aesthetic: what one wants of a novel is either life, in Dreiser's sense, or what art makes of life. Dreiser imposes the decision on us.

For years he had been collecting news stories about young men who had tried to extricate themselves by violence from transient love affairs like his own with Sara White. He was particularly fascinated by the case of one Chester Gillette, who, back in 1906, had chosen to murder rather than marry his pregnant working-girl sweetheart. Current newspapers had followed Gillette's capture, trial, appeal, and execution industriously. A general outline of events and no little detail were there for Dreiser to appropriate.

World War I appears to have deferred the start of the writing. Like many Americans of German blood he was disturbed and uncertain of his sympathies; his participating in the debates between intellectuals that preceded the entry of the United States into the war suggests the extent of his preoccupation. He could, and did, bring together and publish collections of short stories, plays, and essays, but it is reasonable to assume that he had no stomach for undertaking a long piece of work. He waited until 1919.

The procedure could not be quite the one he had used for Yerkes-Cowperwood, since this time he needed some changes in the central character: the Gillette of the newspapers had to be made more passive, less decisive and brutal; incident had to be manipulated so as to intensify the tragedy; the hero had to dream of success but be frustrated by nature, weakness of character, and sex.

Not that Clyde Griffiths' dream is at all complex. He is not bright enough to think out what he wants. In its elementary form, the dream consists of rising in business until you can have the money, luxuries, pleasures, and, especially, women you want – "a good time," as Clyde thinks of it; "the better things," according to Dreiser. Clyde would like to be like his uncle, who owns a factory in Lycurgus, N.Y., or like his cousin, who will one day inherit it and meanwhile drives a car of his own. He would like to sport about with a wealthy, glamorous girl like Sondra Finchley. For wanting nothing better than this he ends in the electric chair.

His parents are street preachers who run a "mission" in Kansas City, and who live a grubby and mean life; they are rigidly religious and dirt poor. He leaves school as soon as he can, and eventually gets a bellhop's job in a flashily luxurious hotel. The glamour he sees about him is everything home isn't. Dimly he wants something like it for himself, just as he wants to play about with the other bellhops and their girls. The fun ends abruptly when a group of them make off with a car for a joyride and manage to run down a small child. Clyde has to disappear.

The early version in which Dreiser drew so many details from his own youth had to be abandoned, but the finished text reveals all the familiar patterns of his family life. In addition to the parents, the pregnant sister, and the rest, there is especially the boy who wants something better than he has been born to. After Dreiser-Hurstwood, Dreiser-Cowperwood, and Dreiser-Witla, now comes Dreiser-Clyde – but for luck and a few chemicals.

Working in a club in Chicago, Clyde meets his father's successful brother, whom he persuades to try him in a job at the factory in Lycurgus, near Utica. In Lycurgus the Griffithses are people of standing; they do as little for this unimpressive relative as decency requires. Clyde lives in drab lodgings, works at a monotonous job, watches his young cousins and their friends from a distance, and learns how wide a gap money can create. He is desperately lonely, but determined to win acceptance.

Here the story falls into another familiar pattern. Loneliness prevails over ambition, and he begins what he intends to be a passing affair with Roberta Alden, a farm girl who has come to work in the factory. She is his reality; the dream remains one of sharing the life of the local smart set and having a girl like glittering Sondra Finchley. By the time he learns that the group is beginning to accept him because Sondra finds him interesting, he learns, also, that Roberta is pregnant.

When she insists on marriage, Clyde panics at the loss of his evaporated dream. Other expedients failing, he forms a half-baked plan of contriving an accident and lures her to a lonely lake in the Adirondacks. Actually the accident that occurs is genuine: Roberta rises in their rowboat and lurches toward Clyde; he hits her unintentionally with his camera; they overturn; a gunwale strikes her on the head and she drowns. Clyde leaves her in the water, wanders about the country awhile, and then joins his rich friends at their summer resort.

His movements have been so inept that the law traces him easily to Lycurgus and back, turning up new evidence at every stop. Clyde is held for murder. An ambitious district attorney has done his work well: letters Clyde has forgotten to destroy, marked travel folders, his behavior where the couple stopped on their way to the lake, what he took with them in the rowboat, and the transparent falsehood of the story Clyde's lawyers cook up for him combine to hide the one fact that might save his life: that he had lost the will, or the nerve, to kill her before Roberta stood up in the boat. The jury finds guilt in the first degree. When both his appeal and a plea to the governor fail, Clyde is executed.

Many readers have complained that Part III of this novel, devoted to the events that follow the drowning, is too long and too painful. But given Dreiser's intention, what else was possible? As is entirely clear at the end, everything in the story is pointed, from the beginning, toward the electric chair. Clyde is caught by his family's circumstances, by his ignorance and inexperience, by his unintelligence, and most of all by his dream of success. Roberta's pregnancy is almost an afterthought of fate. This trap is a machine, and it is of the essence that its movement should not accelerate: it needn't hurry for fear of losing its victim. It is in Part III that we realize fully how unaccidental the seeming accidents of Clyde's life have been.

Actually the trap is life itself. For some years Dreiser had been deeply interested in the work of Jacques Loeb, the physiologist whose studies of elementary forms had led him to the conclusion that any life is a simple matter of mechanics. Expose a flower to light, a chemical change takes place within the plant tissues, and the flower turns its head. Dreiser not only read Loeb's writings but also corresponded with him, and with passing time turned from the determinism of "laws" and "forces" he had learned from the nineteenth-century British toward a mechanistic position of his own. If life in a plant or a fruit fly can be explained as the functioning of a machine, then why not the more complex forms of life and ultimately the universe as a whole? Loeb himself had recommended to psychologists that they investigate the chemical bases of behavior. Years afterward Dreiser was still warmly interested in what Loeb had done. It would be hard to doubt that the theory of mechanism stirred his imagination when he was writing *An American Tragedy* and affected his basic, visceral feeling of life. Not only is Clyde Griffiths caught in a machine, he is a machine — or part of a universal one.

The paradox of *An American Tragedy* is, of course, that machines do not weep over their condition.

Henry James complains because Flaubert confided the role of "central moral consciousness" to such "mean" and uninteresting characters as Emma Bovary and Frédéric Moreau. Obviously the same criticism would apply to Dreiser's novel – if it were indeed true that the only people with a story worth telling are those gifted with intelligence fine enough to understand the moral implications of what happens to, and around, them. Clyde Griffiths is just not morally conscious. Like most of the population of Dreiser's novels, he lives on a plane where moral alternatives aren't visible. He never perceives the tawdriness of his dream of success. In a sense, Dreiser manages to place the moral consciousness not in a character, and not in the omniscient narrator, but in the reader.

However repellent a free animal may be, in a trap it becomes an object of pity. Pity is the dominant emotion of *An American Tragedy*, not for Clyde alone, but for the mother who writes sob-sister reports of his trial so that she can earn the money to be there and goes on an improvised lecture tour to raise more money for the appeal; and for the poor, ignorant farmers who are the parents of Roberta Alden; and for Roberta herself; even for Clyde's weak, incompetent father; and for the poor, dumb victims of the American Dream, everywhere.

The nice critics who complain that to win us over Dreiser has to appeal to the morbid fascination that keeps us panting over the daily accounts of sensational murder trials may not be wholly wrong. But what has Clyde done worse than believe, however dumbly, what he has been taught to believe, and want what he was supposed to want: money, the kind of life one sees more fortunate people lead, love? His excuse is Eugene Witla's: if American life had proposed less sleazy satisfactions he would have aimed at them. In this sense only, the title of this novel is appropriate. Clyde may be cubits beneath the stature of a tragic hero, but America is big enough to have a tragic flaw.

Judged by standards much less stringent than we apply to James and Flaubert, *An American Tragedy* is not a well-made novel. Even H. L. Mencken, for years Dreiser's stout supporter – and who had vigorously defended the earlier novels – found it too long and rambling. It puts many burdens on its reader; the dialogue is awkward; the pace is slow. In contrast, the other great American novel whose hero is killed by his dream of success is written in neatly constructed scenes, and has Nick Carraway in it to judge it for us and to tell Jay Gatsby that he is finer than the Buchanans. But one doesn't finish *The Great Gatsby* with sorrow in one's heart. Neatness may not be the ultimate criterion.

Actually, Dreiser's craftsmanship is of a higher order than his critics willingly admit. His basic procedure has to be situational irony, since so much of the effect depends on the reader's understanding better than the characters do what is happening to them. Hence the valuc of a structure of parallel incidents: the pregnancy of Clyde's sister in the early part and Roberta's pregnancy; the accidental death of the child the joyriders run down and the accident on the lake; the similar scenes with which the novel opens and closes, with the Griffiths family out evangelizing on the sidewalk. Such examples can be multiplied indefinitely. Other ironies are produced by Clyde's wrong estimates of people: his models among the bellhops in Kansas City, whom he takes for experienced men of the world, the reader recognizes as uncouth louts; the uncle he considers a tycoon is in truth a timid small-town businessman somewhat overawed by big-city surroundings; Sondra, his dream woman, actually expresses the full content of her mind in the most repulsive baby talk. For the sake of irony Dreiser is even willing to stretch credibility severely: the farmer from whom Clyde asks directions when he is out driving with his rich friends turns out to be the father of Roberta. With these he devises parallels of language and echoes, such that his reader is reminded of earlier incidents when he learns of later ones, which create something like a fabric of constant cross-reference. How carefully Dreiser planned his work must be obvious. A novel about confused characters, as one critic has said of this one, is not necessarily a confused novel.

At fifty-five, Dreiser had become a public figure. His attitude toward any matter of general interest became news. He had never been one to avoid exposure. The essays of *A Traveler at Forty* (1913), the miscellany called *Hey Rub-a-Dub-Dub* (1920), and *A Book about Myself* (1922) had exhibited his personality, directly or indirectly, from various angles. Now *Dawn* revealed the story of his youth, with great frankness and occasional charm, but also with perceptible self-indulgence. Over the years he had inclined increasingly toward socialism – which may be why society seems more clearly at fault in *An American Tragedy* than in the earlier novels – and he now became repeatedly involved in conspicuous liberal causes.

Few seem to have found his personality a winning one. He made heavy demands on his friends and was easily hurt by them, even when they had been as generous as Arthur Henry and H. L. Mencken. Dreiser and Henry had met in Toledo, where the latter was on the staff of the *Blade*, and the friendship had blossomed rapidly. Henry invited Dreiser and Sara to spend the summer of 1899 in Maumee, where, with Henry's encouragement, Dreiser began *Sister Carrie*. Henry helped revise the manuscript; scholars even believe that some of the holograph is in his hand. Later he aided Dreiser to find work in New York and advised him in his dealings with Doubleday. Relations remained warm until 1904, when Dreiser spent part of his vacation as Henry's guest on an island in Long Island Sound. Henry was between marriages, and Dreiser may not have taken to the new lady. Whatever the cause, he became an awkward companion and put a grave strain on his welcome. Henry, doubtless annoyed, made him a character in a novel, *An Island Holiday*; Dreiser recognized the unflattering portrait and the friendship ended for all time.

With Mencken his relationship lasted longer – from 1907 until Mencken reviewed *An American Tragedy* – and the rift between them was later patched up, but the pattern is similar. The men corresponded cordially for years. Mencken was generous with advice and helpful with ideas. He praised Dreiser's books privately and in print, and stormed at the critics who neglected them. But one unfavorable review was enough to cancel everything. As still other friends, like the British publisher Grant Richards, had learned, the kinder one was to Dreiser the easier it was to wound him.

His stands on foreign affairs were timed as if he wanted them to be unpopular: he delayed condemning the Nazis until after his countrymen had done so almost unanimously; he persisted in trying to join the Communist party – which rejected his applications so long as Earl Browder had a say in its affairs – years after the Russo-German nonaggression pact of 1939 had disabused American liberals about the idealism of the Kremlin. Even favorable critics thought him wrongheaded.

Abstract thinking had never been his forte. His year at Indiana University had not taught him to read critically. He never learned to distinguish science from pseudo-science. Students detect echoes of Herbert Spencer, for example, in his novels, mixed with fragments of psychological theory according to which dwelling on pleasant or unpleasant thoughts induces the formation of corresponding "anastates" and "katastates" in the psyche. This he had culled from the writings of a certain Elmer Gates, who practiced "psychology and psychurgy" in Chevy Chase, Maryland. As he grew older his respect for science seems only to have increased, but what he said about it only added to his reputation for confused thinking.

The truth was that he had grown old. His friends were dying off. His own health was failing. He was no longer sure of the quality of what he wrote. Yet, almost despite himself, he would finish *The Stoic* and *The Bulwark.*

The story of *The Bulwark* had been in his mind since 1912, when a Pennsylvania Quaker girl, Miss Anna Tatum, had told him about her father's grief over his children's departure from the strict Quaker faith. He had drafted occasional bits of it, but invariably put the drafts aside to work on more pressing subjects. Now in old age he took it up again, turning out a novel that may betray some loss of powers – it is briefer and less loaded with detail than his other stories – but is probably the neatest and sharpest of his novels, and humanly a very touching one.

Solon Barnes is a Quaker and follower of the Inner Light who comes from humble beginnings on a Maine farm to a place of power in a Philadelphia bank, acquiring without loss to his integrity the wife, home, family, and respect of his neighbors which are the fruits of success. A crisis comes when he sees that his colleagues in the bank are following practices which, while within the law, remind confirmed readers of Dreiser of Cowperwood. Guided by the Inner Light, and firm in his principles, he resigns from the bank and retires to his family. But the very principles that have sustained him have opened a gulf between him and his children. He has been rigid and authoritarian. One daughter, embittered by her physical homeliness, finds what satisfaction she can in being an assistant to a professor of psychology at Llewellyn College for Women. The other, like Miss Tatum, abandons the quiet Quaker life for the bohemia of Greenwich Village. His son Orville turns into one of those cautiously conservative success seekers Dreiser could never abide. His second son, caught in an escapade that results in the death of a girl, commits suicide in jail. Then his beloved wife, who has stood by him through everything, dies. Seeing how old he is and in what wavering health, and how much he needs them, his daughters come home to be with him – and discover that he has become a man at peace. He has learned to accept his virtues and his faults in humility. When he dies the Quakers call him the Bulwark of their faith.

On one of his last walks through his rural property, Barnes comes on a small puff adder which, in its fright, rises up like a small cobra. He talks quietly to the tiny snake and it relaxes. Later it slithers fearlessly away across the toe of one of his shoes. The old man is deeply stirred, as his daughters see when he tells them of what happened. Barnes, and Dreiser, have moved out of the world of Frank Cowperwood and his lobster into one where the ultimate verity is not that each order of life preys on the one below it. Life does live on life, he muses as he watches an insect eat a leaf, but this must be part of a universal plan – an order in another sense, corresponding to the feeling of order within him.

That Dreiser's mind dwelt much on such ultimately religious questions in his last years would be clear in any case from the concluding pages of *The Stoic,* where Berenice listens to the teaching of the guru. But whereas in that novel the pages come as a puzzling intrusion, *The Bulwark* is something very rare, especially in American literature – a religious novel of impressive dignity and power.

Thematically, the materials of *The Bulwark* are not new: the family that becomes oppressive, the effect on the children of the father's religious inflexibility, the conflict of moral systems, the meaning of success and the values that constitute it. Three of the children also renew character types that are already familiar. But Dreiser has reversed or displaced his values. Material success is no longer a synonym for succcess in life. Peace of mind, internal harmony, and love are prime satisfactions. The role of the family is not necessarily to frustrate. Nothing can stop the changes brought by passing time, but time itself can bring the understanding that certain fundamental virtues survive.

On December 28, 1945, Dreiser himself died.

Published a year after his death, *The Bulwark* did little to change critical opinion. It was an old man's book, and perhaps a book for old men. And his voice came from a remote past.

Broad sectors of American criticism had resisted him for years. The "New Humanists" of the teens and twenties had deplored what they called his "determinist naturalism" and kept up a defense of established morality that frightened off several publishers besides Doubleday. The James revival of the thirties had attached supreme value to the kind of novel Dreiser was least able to write. His old-fashioned technique didn't lend itself to the vivisection of the "New Criticism." The metropolitan "Liberal Intellectuals" had small patience with a novelist who, they held, wrote poorly because he thought poorly. In the two decades between *An American Tragedy* and *The Bulwark*, a generation of technicians like Faulkner, Hemingway, and Fitzgerald had changed ideas about what could be done with the novel as a form. The increasing trend away from realism, beginning at the end of World War II, probably predisposed younger critics to see Dreiser's novels only as vast accumulations of detail, undigested and unformed by any controlling imagination.

The resistance had never been unanimous, of course. From early on there had been Mencken. V. L. Parrington had admired Dreiser, as is evident from an unfinished chapter in the last volume of his influential *Main Currents in American Thought*. Even when Dreiser's stock was at its lowest, the thoughtful and independent Alfred Kazin broke through the clichés of critical disapproval to do him justice in *On Native Grounds* and again in introductions to the reprints of several of the novels. F. O. Matthiessen, after writing luminously about the Jameses, undertook to write a monograph which would offer a balanced view of Dreiser and, indeed, does so, even though left incomplete by Matthiessen's death. And most recently, Robert Penn Warren, with the combined authority of an eminent novelist and a respected critic, marked Dreiser's centennial with his *Homage to Theodore Dreiser.* It should be added that practicing novelists, from Frank Norris to Scott Fitzgerald, James T. Farrell, John Dos Passos, Saul Bellow, and now Warren, have always been more generous in praise of Dreiser than have their critic contemporaries.

It would be gratifying to report that at long last Dreiser had had his due. But is this the truth? The case may be that, after the years that have elapsed, only those who value his work write about him, while the rest care too little to break silence. Even today the Dreiser monument in Terre Haute commemorates not the novelist but the brother who wrote "On the Banks of the Wabash" and "My Gal Sal." As one English student of America, Marcus Cunliffe, remarks in his brief history of American writing, Dreiser remains a special problem for American readers.

Yet he upset the dictum of Henry James, that American life is too thinly textured and culturally unvaried to support the novel, and showed, indirectly, that James was merely indicating the limits of the novel of manners. He shared with Edgar Lee Masters and Sherwood Anderson the somewhat elegiac feeling that even the anonymous, average – or perhaps sub-average – American had his own poignant and significant story. The everyday ordinariness of his people makes his so-called naturalism very different from that of Frank Norris. Norris' notion of naturalism emphasized the abnormal character – Vandover, McTeague – treated in realistic detail but seen through the sensibility of the romantic, and thus infallibly as material for melodrama. Dreiser's people have absolutely nothing of "the beast within," and are not monsters: no Dreiser character, for example, has the innate malevolence of S. Behrman, whose ominous shadow darkens the action of *The Octopus*. For Dreiser, human affairs are always of human size, even when they involve the "Titan," Frank Cowperwood. What happens to the people in his novels could happen to anyone.

Consequently he brought our naturalistic novel into closer similarity to European realism than to the theory-bound oeuvre of Zola. For all of Dreiser's interest in science, science has nothing directly to do with the interest of his stories. The physical environments of his characters aren't animal habitats in the biological sense so much as human situations. As he was deeply aware, himself, he looks back to Balzac.

Yet his achievement is different in nature from Balzac's. Dreiser's novels don't attempt to picture a society or account for the way it works. If he was aware of the broad variety of human types that constitute a world, he made no attempt to represent the variety in his books. Even the most indulgent of his adherents must admit that the secondary figures derive their interest less from what they are than from their relationships to the principals. Pushing the similarity with Balzac too far obscures the basic fact that Dreiser was a master of case histories.

Failure to draw some such distinction has led European readers to assume not only that these cases are typically American, and fully representative of American life, but also that there is little more to American life than what they represent. Marxist critics in particular have used Dreiser's novels as a stick for beating their effigy of American capitalism, holding capitalism responsible for the monotonous cultural poverty to which the novels testify. In the eyes of no few serious students of American literature in the European universities, who forget that when Dreiser finally had some free money, after *An American Tragedy*, he found little better to do with it than play the stock market, he figures among "the artisans of revolt."

Granting that a constant concern with money is an identifying trait of realistic fiction everywhere, Dreiser's realism is set apart by the exclusiveness of the concern. His perspective on life is relentlessly economic: even the artist, Witla, struggles for economic status, and this is true of the rest of his characters whether they concentrate on amassing fortunes or on staying out of the almshouse. Apart from sex, they have few other occupations; they rarely play or indulge in any other gratuitous activity; leisure, to occupy or be bored with, seems foreign to their natures — as indeed does the notion of enjoyment.

The perspective could not but be conditioned by his own experience of life. By birth he belonged to the disadvantaged; in a family that had left an old culture behind without acquiring a new one, and in a rural area, his chances of getting a broader view were small. Nor could such education as he got help greatly. The point is often made that he was among the first American writers whose perspective wasn't that of the East Coast and whose blood wasn't that of the "old stock." This is partly true at best, and perhaps misleading to boot; what is surely relevant is that he grew up in cultural and financial poverty. He tells in *Dawn* of having been sent home from school because the weather was getting cold and he had no shoes.

On this point again he contrasts sharply with Norris, who looks poverty in the eye nowhere in his novels. Vandover loses some inherited wealth, but because of an advancing pathological condition; McTeague's rage for gold is again pathological; the people forced off their ranches are threatened by pauperdom, but we see only two of them suffer its effects, and only briefly, at the very end. At the age when he undertook serious writing, Norris had lived comfortably in London and Paris, and studied at Berkeley and Harvard; Dreiser, at the same age, had barely made it from Terre Haute and Chicago to New York.

By consensus, his most durable novels are those of which he

knew the subjects most intimately: *Sister Carrie, Jennie Gerhardt, An American Tragedy*. Obviously he was just as familiar with the materials of *The "Genius,"* but in this instance the distance between author and subject is wrong. Few critics maintain that the Cowperwood trilogy is of the same quality; one sees so much of Cowperwood, over so many years, and in situations that can't help being repetitious, that unless one shares Dreiser's curiosity about the techniques of fast dealing his hero becomes somewhat too predictable and thus monotonous.

Taken together, these novels don't offer a picture *of* American life so much as pictures *from* American life. The most successful focus on people who start at a disadvantage in the universal competition of a society that substitutes a theoretical social mobility for class distinctions. In this matter of subject Dreiser was not innovating, of course: at least sporadically, the realists of the nineties, especially Crane and Norris, had recognized the interest of such lives as an area for fiction to explore. Dreiser's originality is that, as a native of the area, he could write about life in it without sounding as if he had gone on a slumming expedition. It was in this that he set the example to be followed by the realists of the years between the publication of *An American Tragedy* and World War II – Steinbeck, Farrell, Dos Passos, and the others.

What made him unpopular for a long time was also what made him the kind of novelist he was, that naive innocence of vision that made him report what he saw rather than what he was supposed to see. Good and bad were words; what counted in reality was strength or weakness. Free will was a word; people as he saw them were helpless against external "forces." Morality was a word; the observable reality was nature. He could not resolve such dilemmas, but he could, and did, refuse to sweep them away. Europeans have long been trying to tell us that this kind of novelist should command more than prefunctory respect.

Selected Bibliography

Works of Theodore Dreiser

Sister Carrie. New York: Doubleday, Page, 1900.
Jennie Gerhardt. New York: Harper, 1911.
The Financier. New York: Harper, 1912.
A Traveler at Forty. New York: Century, 1913.
The Titan. New York: John Lane, 1914.
The "Genius." New York: John Lane, 1915.
Plays of the Natural and Supernatural. New York: John Lane, 1916.
A Hoosier Holiday. New York: John Lane, 1916.
Free and Other Stories. New York: Boni and Liveright, 1918.
The Hand of the Potter. New York: Boni and Liveright, 1918.
Twelve Men. New York: Boni and Liveright, 1919.
Hey Rub-a-Dub-Dub. New York: Boni and Liveright, 1920.
A Book about Myself. New York: Boni and Liveright, 1922. Republished as *Newspaper Days*. New York: Horace Liveright, 1931.
The Color of a Great City. New York: Boni and Liveright, 1923.
An American Tragedy. 2 vols. New York: Horace Liveright, 1925.
Moods Cadenced and Declaimed. New York: Boni and Liveright, 1926.
Chains: Lesser Novels and Stories. New York: Boni and Liveright, 1927.
Dreiser Looks at Russia. New York: Horace Liveright, 1928.
A Gallery of Women. New York: Horace Liveright, 1929.
Dawn. New York: Horace Liveright, 1931.
Tragic America. New York: Horace Liveright, 1931.
America Is Worth Saving. New York: Modern Age Books, 1941.
The Bulwark. Garden City, N.Y.: Doubleday, 1946.
The Stoic. Garden City, N.Y.: Doubleday, 1947.

Current American Reprints

An American Tragedy. New York: Signet (New American Library). $1.25.
The Financier. New York: Signet. $1.25.
The "Genius." New York: Signet. $1.50.
Jennie Gerhardt. New York: Dell. $.75.
Sister Carrie. New York: Airmont. $.75. New York: Bantam. $.75. Jack Salzman, ed., Indianapolis: Bobbs-Merrill. $1.75. New York: Dell. $.75. Claud

Simpson, ed., Boston: Houghton Mifflin. $1.35. Louis Auchincloss, ed., New York: Merrill. $1.15. Donald Pizer, ed., New York: Norton. $2.45. New York: Signet. $.75.

The Titan. New York: Signet. $.75.

Critical and Biographical Studies

Beach, Joseph Warren. *The Twentieth-Century Novel: Studies in Technique.* New York: Appleton-Century-Crofts, 1932. Pp. 321–331.

Campbell, Louise, ed. *Letters to Louise.* Philadelphia: University of Pennsylvania Press, 1959.

Cargill, Oscar. *Intellectual America: Ideas on the March.* New York: Macmillan, 1941. Pp. 107–128.

Elias, Robert H. *Theodore Dreiser: Apostle of Nature.* New York: Alfred A. Knopf, 1949. Emended edition, Ithaca, N.Y.: Cornell University Press, 1970.

——, ed. *Letters of Theodore Dreiser.* 3 vols. Philadelphia: University of Pennsylvania Press, 1959.

Geismar, Maxwell. *Rebels and Ancestors.* Boston: Houghton Mifflin, 1953. Pp. 287–379.

Hicks, Granville. *The Great Tradition.* New York: Macmillan, 1933. Pp. 226–237.

Kazin, Alfred. *On Native Grounds.* New York: Reynal and Hitchcock, 1942. Pp. 78–91.

—— and Charles Shapiro. *The Stature of Theodore Dreiser.* Bloomington: Indiana University Press, 1965.

Lehan, Richard. *Theodore Dreiser, His World and His Novels.* Carbondale: Southern Illinois University Press, 1969.

Matthiessen, F. O. *Theodore Dreiser.* New York: William Sloan, 1951.

Moers, Ellen. *Two Dreisers.* New York: Viking Press, 1969.

Shapiro, Charles. *Theodore Dreiser: Our Bitter Patriot.* Carbondale: Southern Illinois University Press, 1962.

Swanberg, W. A. *Dreiser.* New York: Scribner's, 1965.

Spiller, Robert E., *et al. Literary History of the United States.* Revised edition, New York: Macmillan, 1953. Pp. 1197–1208.

Warren, Robert Penn. *Homage to Theodore Dreiser, August 27, 1871–December 28, 1945, on the Centennial of His Birth.* New York: Random House, 1971.

Walcutt, Charles C. *American Literary Naturalism, a Divided Stream.* Minneapolis: University of Minnesota Press, 1956. Pp. 180–221.